Interactive Press

Tuning Wordsworth's Piano

Jane Simpson grew up in New Zealand in a home filled with art and lively debate. Her art-educator parents emigrated from England just after she was born. She has a PhD (Otago) in religion and gender in NZ (1939–59) and has taught social history and religious studies in universities in Australia and New Zealand. Her poems and academic articles have been published in books, anthologies and journals both within New Zealand and internationally, including *takahē*, *Poetry New Zealand* and *Meniscus*. Her chapbook, *Candlewick kelp*, was published by Poets Group in 2002, and her first full-length collection, *A world without maps*, by Interactive Publications in 2016. She has an adult son, and currently teaches academic writing as a Senior Tutor at Lincoln University.

I0224241

Interactive Press
The Literature Series

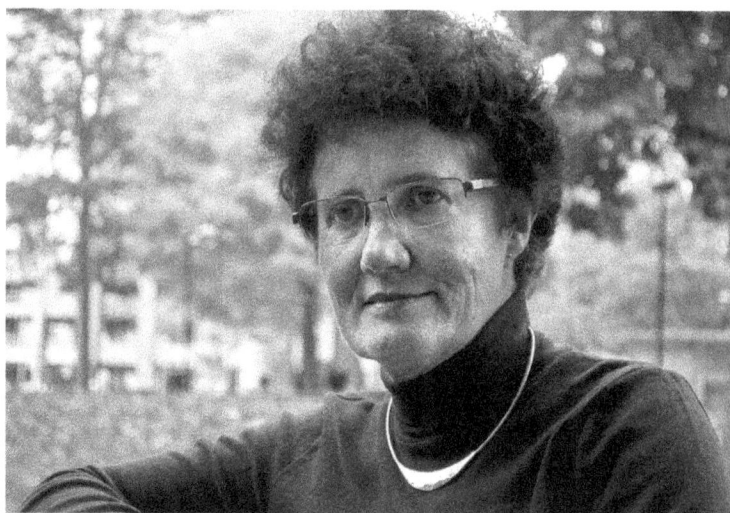

Tuning Wordsworth's Piano

Jane Simpson

Interactive Press
an imprint of IP (Interactive Publications Pty Ltd)
Treetop Studio • 9 Kuhler Court
Carindale, Queensland, Australia 4152
ipoz.biz/interactive-press
ipoz.biz/ipstore

First published by IP in 2019

Printed in 12 pt Adobe Garamond Pro on 14 pt Avenir Book.

ISBN 9781925231915 (PB); ISBN 9781925231922 (eBook)

A catalogue record for this book is available from the National Library of Australia

To my father

ACKNOWLEDGEMENTS

Cover image: Zoltan Tarlac, Dreamstime.com, detail from the original painting by Robert Delaunay, *Simultaneous Contrasts: Sun and Moon*, Paris, 1913, Museum of Modern Art, New York.

Front cover design: Francis Ahlers-Simpson

Author photo: James Shanly

Book design: David P. Reiter

Some of these poems have appeared in *Poetry New Zealand* and *takahē*. Two poems from the Catlins sequence were published in the New Zealand Poetry Society's anthologies, *after the cyclone* (2017) and *The unnecessary invention of punctuation* (2018). 'Undercover' was shown in *Our land and water* (2018), a touring exhibition organised by the National Science Challenge programme.

Many of the poems have been aired at the annual series of readings organised by the Canterbury Poets' Collective. I am grateful to members for their encouragement, particularly Jeni Curtis and Gail Ingram. Some of the poems were first read in the weekly te reo Māori services at the Transitional Cathedral, Christchurch.

Special thanks to Joanna Preston for her rigour as an editor; to Tony Beyer for his comments on this collection and *A world without maps*; to Bernie Hall for strong links with my family through art, poetry and theology; to the late Vivian Lynn for her work and generosity in sharing about her art practice.

Grateful thanks to the curators of the Christchurch Art Gallery / Te Puna o Waiwhetū, for their discussion of modernism in New Zealand landscape painting; to Cilla McQueen and Hone Tuwhare for their poetry of place. Thanks to Christchurch Central Librarians for recent literature on the Catlins and its communities.

When I despaired at finding Hone Tuwhare's crib at Kākā Point, I stumbled across Gary Wynyard, son of one of his closest friends. The next day he kindly took me to where Hone had lived and worked. As I stood in front of his crib, the wind howling, and read from my own book, I felt I had come home.

Contents

III

I

Tuning Wordsworth's piano

Unspoilt Nature is nature writ too small;
nature at our feet;
nodding daffodils saying 'Yes',
green the obverse of grey paths
in the Victorian Botanical Gardens
where children cavort and disks wheel,
Orphic artists paint concentric circles,
create the sun – sing the music
of the spheres.

Under cover

(for Alexis)

Mushrooms, delicate as lace,
take over where gardeners
have reduced summer's riot
– orange irises, golden rod,
and annuals with Latin names
too numerous to remember –
to stubble on the battlefield
of the Botanical Gardens'
herbaceous border.

A student flat, in a Christchurch winter

The flames entertained us, better
than any television set
in the days of black and white,
stoned, zoned out
making shapes from flames, like
people with crooked noses
in the clouds, or the man in the moon.
Philip Clairmont's hessian fireplace
hangs from nails in the Christchurch Art Gallery,
full of demonic eyes
and flames licking,
painted under artificial light.

Threatening rain

(after Kim Addonizio)

Lining up its heavy clouds,
a brainstorm on a poem
scatters ideas across the Canterbury sky,
as the nor'west presses down on the city.

A brainstorm on a poem,
signature cumulus lenticular form,
as the nor'west presses down on the city.
Over the Plains women draw curtains, retreat inside.

Signature cumulus lenticular form.
No escaping Te Hau Kai Tangata;
over the Plains women draw curtains, retreat inside
under a sky threatening rain all day.

No escaping Te Hau Kai Tangata;
the wind warning death is near
under a sky threatening rain all day,
darkening, then brightening.

The wind warning death is near
scatters ideas across the Canterbury sky,
darkening, then brightening,
lining up its heavy clouds.

From a bed of stars

Rain beads on brassicas,
the meniscus, taut

between white veins, is a jewel
that reflects the beloved,

would reflect the Milky Way
were it not for the snap

of ice on opened leaves.

Rewarewa

taken from your grove
can you thrive, alone, in the city?

Rewarewa, grain like a river,
sold in a black planter bag.

Rewarewa, where do I plant you,
taken from under the forest canopy?

Rewarewa, frost tender, your leaves are
sharp and jagged, yet you tickle my ungloved hands.

Do I bring you inside for the winter,
or let you declare yourself – frost-cloth or not,

like the Rewarewa at the corner
of the Gasson Street Guruji Supermarket?

From Leonardo to Dürer

Where do your eyes fix – empty
yet alive the more I look,
a poet's stare, the mouth downturned,
a noble nose, a prophet's hair –
Isaiah, maybe.
Shadow and form, beard
once red, drawn in red chalk,
thinning, sinuous as engraved copper.

What do historians say? Made
in your image, a portrait of sadness,
brooding over scattered
geometry, a sphere and instruments
of measurement.

Three ways to prepare a veggie garden

Buy a house surrounded
by concrete, soil soured by time,
needing pig slurry and steaming sawdust
prescribed by the old professor, then
dig the goodness in

or rent an allotment, leave it
fallow, see what pierces through
unprepossessing clay – asparagus spikes,
onion spears – perennials
decoration around the edge

or you can knock down
the front wall, dig out the gnarled
camellia by the street,
sow pellets of blue
lupins, wait till Spring
then destroy the sea of
flowers, swaying
chest high, shred their stalks
to nothing, and leave
prehensile roots
to rot in the ground.

Still life

silverbeet in rows, shooting stars from damp soil
everlasting spinach unexposed to sunlight
a speculum, warm as a crab
a marriage bed for the homeless
camembert and crackers deep in a pannier
a lacquered bowl, chipped, like memories

to the cove

(after Airini Beautrais)

to the heft
to the heave
to the coast
to the crest

to the lip
to the lap
to the spill
to the spume

to the float
to the fizz
to the wind
to the melt

to the toss
to the hurl
to the hush
to the lost

II

The patina of summers

cycling the Catlins

With wing feathers trailing
(for Gary)

I

Wind, surf and jokes drown out
my tentative 'tēnā kotou'. They laugh,
another cyclist lost, looking on the flat
for the Kākā Point camping ground.
They point to the top
of the hill, invite me

to come on up
through their property.

The reason
I'm here – a pilgrim
to a poet's unmarked crib.

II

At dawn I see
his *bacon-rasher sky*
fried eggs coming up

leave unladen
for Tokatā Nugget Point
where Royal Spoonbills nest
in a scruffy tree.

III

Divers appear from a hidden bay –
brothers from the whānau,
empty-handed.

They send me on ahead, down the hill.
I am a ship in full sail, the wind
on my back a Celtic blessing.

It was reo all night, down at the pub,
Hone and Dad. Did they go on!
Whisky kept them warm
in their draughty cribs.

His crib is ravaged, but the reo alive –
father tongue / mother tongue.

Unmarked crib

The sou'west exhausts all adjectives
at Hone's crib,

his writing shed smooth
as a fridge, held fast
with a lock, and key left in.

Lean-tos encrust the house.
A lull then a gift – a wind
that blows kisses over weatherboards
bearded with lichen.

The storm leaves love bites,
broken palings a hasty repair –
mark the spot with an x.

Talking point

The kākā at Kāka Point
is a curiosity in the museum
of the pub. Stuffed, it perches
next to the diploma,
an honorary doctorate, on display,
which Hone Tuwhare dedicated with love
For the Foreshore Café
in his hallmark cursive hand.

The kākā of Kākā Point once
gossiped, flashed their feathers.
Farms split their forests, broke up
their chatter, banished
their antics.

The lone female in the aviary
at the Dunedin Botanic Gardens
beats her wings
in a narrow space,
back and forth, back
and forth.
Then I hear her chatter.

In the long grass at his crib

I'm reading to Hone
but he has returned to his tīpuna

I'm reading a poem to Hone
but he's buried in his family's urupā

I'm reading a poem of my own to Hone
but there's nothing of him left at his crib

I'm reading a poem of my own from my new book to Hone
the wind howls – now he is listening to me.

Folios upended at Nugget Point

He wāhi huihui o Papa tūānuku,
o Takaroa, o Tāwhirimātea,
meeting place
of rock and waves, wind and tide

The wind was witness
when layers were tilted up from the sea,
when seas shaped Te Wai Pounamu's coasts
and broke up its headlands.
At Tokatā, tempest and surge
left islands as evidence – folios of rock, edges
uncut, bound together by time.

Who are the rūnanga
who placed these memorials here?
Stone by stone, frame by frame, I move down
a narrow path around a colonial headland.

Decoding CH14, Ōwaka, after Rātānui

greenist green
our native forest
medium green
is patterned exotic
scrub
simply is

white fits
no pre-existing
category
any of the six
on the 88-
item key

illuminated from
a northeast sun
straddles
contours
shades into grey
not defined

is not
radiance
in itself
but apophatic
saying
unsaying

not among
the miscellaneous
cartographer's
grab bag
of human
interventions

fence
reservoir covered
isolated building
shipwreck
telephone
line

white is other
though familiar
the legend
a ledger
of profit
and loss

high
on the Hinahina Hill
fine
black lines
speak
on white's behalf

Ōwaka to
Papatōwai
unkeyed white is
exotic
unirrigated
pasture

21

The language for forests

is the language of dress
    where nouns are also verbs
in active and passive voice –

native forest is a blanket
    of shifting green,
bush blankets the hills and
    rata the canopy, or
the hills are blanketed
    red at Christmas time.

Papatūānuku throws her cloak
    at a precise angle down to Tahakopa Bay.
Podocarps cloak the lowlands
    that escaped the milling era.
The information sign explains
    why the forest is cloaked as it is.

*

The language for forests
    is the language of sex,
passive and active –

male and female, side by
    side, dioecious kahikatea
left untouched at scenic spots –
    outlived their seedlings,
hung their heads
    over virgin bush.

*

Sex and power, a political act
    of the North in the South;
the land is a woman
    abused, stripped of her forests
all to make farms, perennial
    ryegrass from valley to ridge.

Descending to the Tahakopa side

Tahakopa Bay
Scenic Reserve

greets me with the cut capitals
of a Government art deco
Tourist Office poster, silkscreened
blue on white.

Crisp edges meet
the gravel, podocarps
are macrocarpas, clipped.
Spinning blades have made
a portal to a slice of curves,
foreshortened beaches,
from Tautuku to Tahakopa,

the descent silent
except for local dialects –
bellbirds and tui, descendants
of those from moa-hunter days,
taught waiata near middens,
scientifically recorded
on maps not for sale.

The map, CH13 Curio Bay

cut up, laminated and folded to fit
says 'The Reservoir'. I can see

a lake, a step on a staircase,
angles and edges out to Haldane Bay,

a slice through estuaries, caught in a glimpse
on Te Waipounamu's southernmost coast,

a distilled McCahon
imposed in an instant, then withdrawn

as I cycle slower than walking pace,
buffeted by the wind.

Behind the pedals the rhythm of settlements visited:
Kākā Point, Ōwaka, Papatōwai – a lexical map.

Campervans rush past to Slope Point,
the minutes and seconds of extremity.

In front of me, ploughed hills are rolling r's,
Rakiura stretches out, blue as a whale.

At the DOC camping ground, Papatōwai

tents are an airfoil, behind wind-clipped kāmahi
at the estuary's edge,
encrustations on caravans, limpets
tensioned with aluminium poles,
a canvas-walled whare kai where

sausages fizz on the patina
of summers,
the roof's thwack
is a bass drum, the biggest
in the orchestra
played by a child, the second
from a second marriage

whose whānau, two hours
from Tokanui, pitch a temporary city,
where chilly bins are treasure chests
of chorizo, camembert and prawn kebabs
shared with a stranger

Waiting, across Foveaux Strait

mist covers   fog screens
cloud wraps   Rakiura
imagined at Waipapa Point,
raked seating for an audience of one.

Levels of sentience separate you, island, from me:
amoeba, plankton, surface scuttlers,
quota, tourist asset, more
than animal.

Rakiura, yearned for as I cycle
from Curio Bay to Fortrose,
is a gap
when shutters open briefly,
a twitch of lace, a ghost,
a gift.

III

Sonnenizio on a line by R. S. Thomas

I have seen the sun break through
and stretch at sunset across evergreen
space, then dress a single holly tree with sunburst berries;
been stopped by stage light flooding a sun-starved city – ginko,
green, blue, indigo – notes on an unsung score; sensed harmony
in sunflowers and the nautilus – the golden mean;
tasted the Son's new wine, pure extravagance, where
once austere theologies were Sunday best.

Did God not put the sunbow in the sky? In an ancient church
the priest wraps hands, two sons are exchanging vows:
what God has joined together let not man put asunder.
Steeple bells are heard beyond the sun and stars.
The sun's absence – scented nights, rumpled air, a couple wed;
men, not the sun, rising from their marriage bed.

Feminine construct

Its workings mysterious tracings,
criss-cross movements

of nuns in action, with
steel-capped boots, needle

and thread. Their prayers
string underwires, take in the slack,

stretching round the copious
breast of God.

Second offenders

(Port Arthur, 1830–76)

Prison was a place of
land broken in – self-sufficient
in the lonely heat.

Re-offend and be sent
to Port Arthur,
wear manacles and be
tormented
by the open sky.

Sit in a stall with blinkers
like horses', see only
the preacher
beating the whip
of the scriptures;
to bring them to mind
back in their cells, at their looms
in silence, like Quakers
at prayer, in the rhythm

of moral reform;
to weave,
to mend, to go
slowly mad.

Lifers were freed
when the colony closed.
Behind unlocked doors
in hospital and asylum,
some grew old, safe
from the society, once safe
from them.

This Good Friday

I shall not go up the aisle at the Cardboard Cathedral
   and kiss the feet of the plaster cast Jesus.
I will not   touch the hands
   of a laser printed icon,
       cup the shoulder
         of an outstretched wooden arm,
       put my hand into his marble side
         gushing tears or
       sense the space behind the fibreglass
       figure of sorrow.

I will see in their place Christa on the Cross
back in the Manhattan Anglican Cathedral, bare
-breasted, sculpted in bronze;
scandalous and true.

Seeing Claire at Evensong

Serrations are scars
and soft flesh
I brush with feather tips
down her arm.

They glisten like the key
-hole slits either side and below
my belly I see every morning
in the shower –

a sacrament of life, body
and blood, my womb
cauterised:
I will not die like my aunt.

I sit next to Claire, see
her scars. She lets me
feel her touch with death –
cuts, slices of crumbly bread.

Sixtieth Pentecost

Chrism slops in the boat
of my hands, on the skin
of a coracle.

Palms form a pan
for mountain streams to swirl
their fines, and specks of gold.

The light of the world
is playing
form and void,

forwards and backwards
in the mirror
of a whare-tent cathedral.

The oily meniscus
quivers with the cross
pressed into hands; folds deep

as a newborn's
wrapped in vernix
from her mother's womb.

The first and the last

(after Vivian Lynn, *The Gates of the Goddess*)

You turn my blood,
my first blood, sin
on a spotless garment,
into every woman's blood.

You turn my blood
into flared wings –
your feathers are
menstrual calendars
on tapa cloth.

Your wings are gates –
the goddess presides, last
period or not.

Not the priest asking:
'How long is it since
your last confession?'
male bleeding
making clean.

In your pavilions
I leave centuries sewn
into days crossed off,

the artist in the gallery,
the goddess within.

Noli me tangere

Frost is a poem etched inside
on glass. Icy symmetries – fearful
to the touch – burn the skin,
before the fire of dawn burns the skies.

In a middle-eastern garden women have come
to tend Jesus' body.
Frozen grass pricks his feet. He waits.

Mary lifts her head at the sound
of his voice, hears him say her name;
Do not touch me he said,
I have not ascended to the Father
yet he let her cup his feet:

no dread omnipotence, ascending through the sky,
leaving Earth to be consumed, suffer, bleed and die.

The cry

Red is the colour of her feet on fire,
her eyes are Goya's flashing terror,
her legs are organ pedals making thunder,
her body is a temple filled with awe and wonder.

She protests at endless pharmacopoeia,
her hands in the grip of an obsessive mirror,
her navel has a PEG to get food in her,
her body is a vessel in fathomless water.

Her illness has defied all attempts at capture;
her mind held hostage, a prisoner to torture.
Yet her rage is brighter than a refiner's fire,
her passion, when kindled, is fearless and tender.

She lives to see her grandson, makes a simple wish:
to tremble at his voice, his manly kiss.

The autumn of nuns

The smell of Latin fills dank woods
where Canonesses of St Augustine
lead girls in procession:

sixth formers from the Continent, juniors
from around the Commonwealth,
and English girls who cried themselves to sleep.

Sister swings the thurible – incense envelops prayer,
the numinous mixes with mist,
leaves reflect light in benediction.

Smell the waft of roses from the cloister.
Almost out of sight, a younger nun kneels
in the sanctuary. Strikes herself with knotted leather cords.

The poetry lesson, air laden – Sister,
her voice mellifluous, censes
her nine-year-olds with sonnets and ballads;

We write our own in response, a silent litany,
remember the sprinkling, layer over layer
of sycamore, ash and oak.

barocca pearl

silverbeet are fluted
columns down a temple wall

spinach is a philosopher king
reclining on a couch

kale are rows of chasubles
freed from ordinary time

and each broccoli is a universe
an immense bouquet of stars

The weight of clothes

Where nurses laid her out, her daughter
lays out her clothes. Her grandson
takes her pictures down,
her husband tips out her drawers.

Back at his house the Advent wreath
announces the time for last things:

to linger over the sheer, red dress
she wore at Christmas parties;

to go through the clothes
she never wore, stuffed
into rubbish bags, forgotten in the loft.

Time to place her tops in piles –
memorable, casual, formal –
spread trousers out from XXS to XL

bundle them up for charities to honour
the generosity of her faith – Catholic
to St Vincent de Paul, ecumenical
to the City Mission.

In Lent, her daughter takes
the best garments out again,
washes mohair, angora cardigans,
merino vests for paper-thin skin.
Clouds of eucalyptus are her prayers
filling the sky.

She goes across town and gives
her finest wool garments
to the softly-spoken Bhutanese,
resettled after fifteen years' exile –
their first winter
in her mother's adopted city.

Spine titles

The Disappearance of God
    for one who felt abandoned.

The Body Adorned in stone
    dancers twisting down temple walls.

Beyond God the Father with its cry of outrage:
    'When God is male, male is God'.

Enough recipe books to make a collection
    the internet has left for dead.

Which second-hand bookshops
    will accept the things

my mother left
    that I have left behind?

Written in honey

The kowhai is a campanile –
each flower a golden bell
bees enter, not a tower marking
the end of wars, but a tree
whose sound is colour,
whose utu the giving and taking
of nectar and pollen.

*

To remember the dead,
the undertaker rests
a seedling kowhai against
the front doorstep of the one
left behind; the promise
of life, in a perfumed
wooden tube.

*

The widower names the seedling
after his wife, keeps her
in the sunniest room through the starkest winter,
plants her facing the street, gazes
on her gold.

*

Spring, summer,
waggle, tremble, dance
in the most radiant language,
before the easterly threshes
the seedpods hanging round
her neck, earrings tossed
in the winds of memory.

Scouring the tidal zone

It nibbled
with green-stained teeth
at his mind. Weeks drew
into months

Roman and Saxon gods forgot
their names; months drew
into years.

The ring of white gold he made
only for her
was lost in the room
she had made her home.

So he bought a new one,
had a piece cut out so it fitted
her shrivelled finger, shrivelled frame.

—*Finders keepers*
two years later
lodged in the toe
of a fleece-lined slipper
—*losers weepers*
buried in her side
of the wardrobe.

He who had never worn a wedding ring
now threaded it onto a chain, wore it
next to his chest – he couldn't say *heart* –
close as she could possibly be.

He left no instructions

so on the way to my father's Requiem
mourners will gather
at the wire-fenced Basilica

his students will come in black suits
with flamboyant shirts, and form a line
in front of the hearse

sip wine from a pool of gold,
hold the chalice and feel
his hammer marks.

*

Remember the outcry

at the Christ stripped
by the sculptor, true to scripture.

See the tapestry made by beating,
hanging heavy behind tabernacle doors.

Look up at the back-to-front Madonna
bringing down the mighty from their thrones
and lifting up the poor

stand and imagine, on the other side
of the containers, a once sacred place,
see his body
that is not his body.

*

in and out of season
bring him lilies.

Notes

Tuning Wordsworth's piano

Orphic artists departed from strict Cubism and joyfully embraced colour. Robert Delaunay used discs of flat colour to make his paintings 'sing', like pure tones in music.

Under cover

This poem is dedicated to a former student, a French research scientist and specialist in the cultivation of edible fungi from New Zealand forests.

A student flat, in a Christchurch winter

Philip Clairmont, *Fireplace*, 1971, acrylic on unstretched hessian. Clairmont (1949–84) was strongly influenced by German expressionism. His early work used frames and mirrors to play with dichotomies between inner and outer worlds.

Threatening rain

After Kim Addonizio's poem 'Darkening, then Brightening'. **Te Hau Kai Tangata** – the Ngāi Tahu name for the nor'west wind. The name used by the earlier Waitaha people, Ma-uru, the clear wind, had no connotations of death.

From Leonardo to Dürer

Leonardo Da Vinci, *Self Portrait in Red Chalk*, Turin Royal Library, 1512.

Albrecht Dürer, *Melencolia I*, engraving, 1514.

With wing feathers trailing

Thanks to Gary, who showed me Hone's crib.

Hone – Hone Tuwhare (Ngāpuhi, 1922–2008) moved to Kākā Point in the Catlins in 1992.

Folios upended at Nugget Point

The epigraph is from a memorial stone on Tokatā Nugget Point, one of a series commemorating the Ngāi Tahu Claims Settlement Act (1998). This reinstated full Ngāi Tahu access to their customary food gathering and preserving areas, lost in Otago in 1864 with the advent of organised colonisation.

Decoding CH14, Ōwaka, after Rātānui

CH14, Ōwaka – a topographical map.

apophatic – a type of theological thinking in which negation is used; God is described in terms of what God is not, such as invisible.

The language for forests

dioecious kahikatea – kahitakea trees are either male or female, most apparent in Spring, when the male is covered with brown cones and the female with blue ovules.

Second offenders

The penal colony at Port Arthur reflected changes in British penal policy, from the use of physical restraint to Quaker-influenced 'humane' methods, including segregation and absolute silence by all inmates.

This Good Friday

Christa – sculpted by British artist Edwina Sandys in 1975, is the first representation of a female Christ on the Cross. It was first shown in London in 1975, then in the Cathedral Church of St John the Divine in Manhattan in 1984. The sculpture was removed after protests that it was historically and theologically indefensible. In 2016 *Christa* was welcomed back.

Sixtieth Pentecost

chrism – the holy oil used by priests in the ministry of healing to anoint the sick; a sacramental action used at the onset of an illness, in times of crisis and before surgery.

whare-tent cathedral – the roof shape of the distinctive Cardboard Cathedral, Christchurch, designed by Shigeru Ban, the award-winning Japanese 'emergency' architect, following the destruction of the city's former Anglican Cathedral in the 22 February 2011 earthquake.

The first and the last

Based on Vivian Lynn's installation, *Gates of the Goddess – a southern crossing attended by the Goddess*, 1986, Govett-Brewster Gallery, New Plymouth.

tapa – cloth made from bark throughout the Pacific, often highly decorated.

Noli me tangere

The Latin for the phrase in John 20:17, spoken by Jesus to Mary Magdalene when she recognised him after his resurrection.

The cry

Goya – this refers to the painting by Spanish artist Francisco Goya, *The Third of May 1808* (1814) showing an execution by firing squad. It is seen as a ground-breaking, archetypal image of the horrors of war.

pharmacopoeia – an official publication containing a list of medicinal drugs with their effects and directions for their use.

PEG – Percutaneous Endoscopic Gastrostomy, a procedure in which a patient is fed directly into the stomach, through a flexible feeding tube. Fluids and medications can also be given.

The autumn of nuns

numinous – a term coined by German theologian, Rudolph

Otto (1869–1937), to describe the experience of the sacred, as both awe-inspiring and fascinating mystery.

thurible – a metal vessel suspended from chains in which incense is burned. Used in liturgies to cense the congregation.

The weight of clothes

Hindu Bhutanese were persecuted by the majority Buddhist population and fled to Nepal. Fifteen years later, in 2007, New Zealand became the first country in the world to accept them as refugees.

Written in honey

utu – a concept in Māori meaning reciprocity, balance and harmony in relationships between individuals and groups. Utu may involve revenge or retribution. Here the meaning is extended to relationships in the wider natural world.

He left no instructions

The wire-fenced Basilica – the Cathedral of the Blessed Sacrament, Christchurch, one of the finest examples of French neo-classic architecture in Australasia, severely damaged in the Canterbury earthquakes of 2010–11.

the Christ stripped by the sculptor – Llew Summers, *Stations of the Cross. XI. Jesus is nailed to the Cross*, marble, 1975. Controversy at the nakedness of Christ led the artist to reluctantly add a plaster loin cloth.

the tapestry – Ida Lough, *Earth with heaven united*, tapestry, 1975.

tabernacle doors – Ria Bancroft, *Christ has died – he is risen*, Tabernacle screen doors, bronze, 1975–76.

The works of art were part of an extensive programme of repair and liturgical renewal in the 1970s. They were commissioned by my father in his role as a member of the Cathedral of the Blessed Sacrament Charitable Trust.

www.ingramcontent.com/pod-product-compliance
Lightning Source LLC
Chambersburg PA
CBHW020218090426
42734CB00008B/1127